D0768584

CALGARY PUBLIC LIBRARY

FEB / / 2008

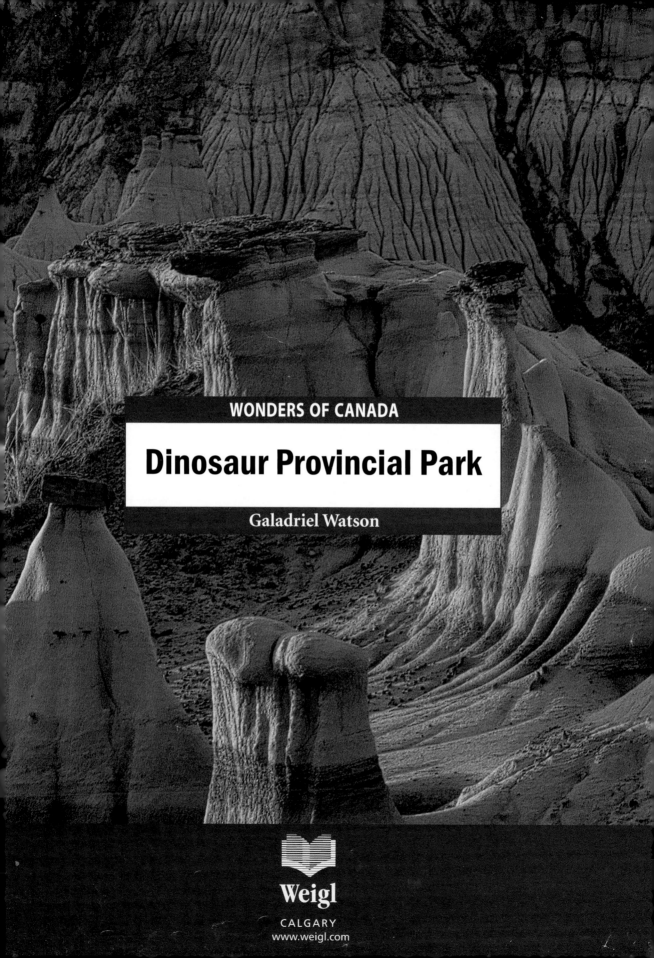

WONDERS OF CANADA

Dinosaur Provincial Park

Galadriel Watson

Weigl

CALGARY
www.weigl.com

Published by Weigl Educational Publishers Limited
6325 10th Street SE
Calgary, Alberta
T2H 2Z9

Website: www.weigl.com
Copyright ©2008 WEIGL EDUCATIONAL PUBLISHERS LIMITED

All rights reserved. No part of this publication may be reproduced, stored in a retrieval system,
or transmitted in any form or by any means, electronic, mechanical, photocopying, recording,
or otherwise, without the prior written permission of the publisher.

We acknowledge the financial support of the Government of Canada through the Book
Publishing Industry Development Program (BPIDP) for our publishing activities.

Library and Archives Canada Cataloguing in Publication

Watson, Galadriel
      Dinosaur Provincial Park / Galadriel Watson.

(Wonders of Canada)
Includes index.
ISBN 978-1-55388-391-3 (bound)
ISBN 978-1-55388-392-0 (pbk.)

      1. Dinosaur Provincial Park (Alta.)--Juvenile literature. 2. World
Heritage areas--Alberta--Juvenile literature. I. Title. II. Series.
FC3665.D56W38 2007   j971.23'4   C2007-902259-6

Printed in the United States of America
1 2 3 4 5 6 7 8 9 0 11 10 09 08 07

Photograph and Text Credits

Every reasonable effort has been made to trace ownership and to obtain permission to
reprint copyright material. The publishers would be pleased to have any errors or omissions
brought to their attention so that they may be corrected in subsequent printings.

© **Alberta Tourism, Parks, Recreation and Culture:** pages 1, 3, 9, and 21 middle; **Glenbow
Archives**: page 19 top (NA-99-2) and 19 bottom left (NA-263-1); Courtesy of **Natural
Resources Canada, Geological Survey of Canada**: page 11 left (Reproduced with the
permission of the Minister of Public Works and Government Services Canada, 2007).

Project Coordinator
Leia Tait

Design
Terry Paulhus

All of the Internet URLs given in the book were valid at the time of publication. However, due
to the dynamic nature of the Internet, some addresses may have changed, or sites may have
ceased to exist since publication. While the author and publisher regret any inconvenience
this may cause readers, no responsibility for any such changes can be accepted by either
the author or the publisher.

Contents

Valley of Bones

Imagine driving across southern Alberta. The highway stretches straight before you. The flat, prairie grassland that lines the road reaches far into the distance. Suddenly, the landscape changes. The road heads down into a valley. **Hoodoos** rise from the ground in fantastical shapes. Steep, striped cliffs reveal ancient rocks. Cave-like sinkholes, deep ruts, and rocks that look like popcorn dot the ground.

This is Dinosaur Provincial Park. Seventy-five million years ago, it was home to some of the world's fiercest dinosaurs. Today, the park is an important **fossil** site. The remains of nearly 40 different dinosaur **species** have been found here. Along with its rich history, the park's mix of **badlands** and giant cottonwood trees make it unlike any other place on Earth. To protect these treasures, Dinosaur Provincial Park was named a World Heritage Site in 1979.

▬ Dinosaur Provincial Park is known for its spectacular scenery. At sunset, rocks in the park appear deep orange, and strange shadows are cast by the park's many unique rock formations.

What is a World Heritage Site?

Heritage is what people inherit from those who lived before them. It is also what they pass down to future generations. Heritage is made up of many things. Objects, traditions, beliefs, values, places, and people are all part of heritage. Throughout history, these things have been **preserved**. A family's heritage is preserved in the stories, customs, and objects its members pass on to each other. Similarly, a common human heritage is preserved in the beliefs, objects, and places that have special meaning for all people, such as Dinosaur Provincial Park.

The United Nations Educational, Scientific and Cultural Organization (UNESCO) identifies places around the world that are important to all people. Some are important places in nature. Others are related to **culture**. These landmarks become World Heritage Sites. They are protected from being destroyed by **urbanization,** pollution, tourism, and neglect.

Hundreds of dinosaur fossils have been found sticking out of the rocks at Dinosaur Provincial Park.

You can learn more about UNESCO World Heritage Sites by visiting **http://whc.unesco.org**.

▶Think about it ◀

World Heritage Sites belong to all people. They provide a link to the past. These sites also help people from many cultures connect with each other. Think about your own heritage. What landmarks are important to you? Think about the places that have shaped your life. Make a list of your personal heritage sites. The list might include your home, your grandparents' home, your school, or any other place that is special to you and your family. Next to each location on the list, write down why it is important to you.

Where in the World?

Dinosaur Provincial Park is located in the province of Alberta. The park is about 50 kilometres northeast of the city of Brooks. It is 225 kilometres east of Calgary, the largest city in Alberta.

Most of Dinosaur Provincial Park is nestled in the Red Deer River Valley. To reach the park, visitors must follow a road about 100 metres into the valley. The Red Deer River winds through the valley, dividing the park into two parts.

Dinosaur Provincial Park covers more than 70 square kilometres. Tourists can visit only about 10 percent of this area. Here, there are camping facilities, walking trails, and the Park Visitor Centre. The rest of the park is closed to protect it from damage. Scientists often venture into the protected areas to study the fossils and landscape. Other visitors can only see these parts of the park on a guided hike or bus tour.

The welcome sign at the entrance to Dinosaur Provincial Park is carved with the outline of a *Corythosaurus*. This is a type of duck-billed dinosaur that once lived in the area.

Puzzler

Provincial parks are areas of land or water that are set aside by the government of a province for protection, education, recreation, or tourism. There are hundreds of provincial parks and protected areas in Alberta. They cover more than 27,500 square kilometres of land and water. Research Alberta's provincial parks on the Internet or at the library. Then, match the letter location markers on the map to the parks listed below.

ANSWERS: 1. B 2. C 3. F 4. A 5. E 6. D

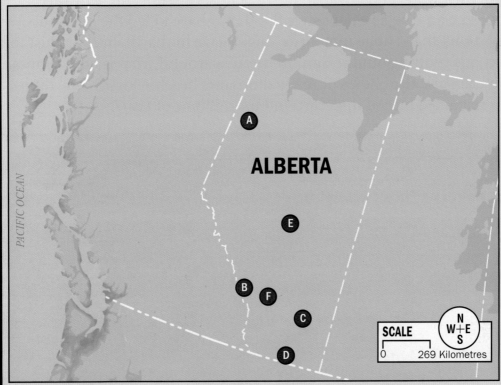

1. Canmore Nordic Centre Provincial Park

2. Dinosaur Provincial Park

3. Fish Creek Provincial Park

4. Historic Dunvegan

5. Lois Hole Centennial Provincial Park

6. Writing-on-Stone Provincial Park

A Trip Back in Time

Seventy-five million years ago, Dinosaur Provincial Park looked very different from how it looks today. It stood near the shoreline of a vast seaway. Lagoons, ponds, swamps, and marshes dotted the land. These were filled with turtles, crocodiles, salamanders, and fish. Giant reptiles swam in the water and flew through the skies. Dinosaurs ruled the land.

Dinosaurs lived in the area that is now Dinosaur Provincial Park for 10 million years. Fierce **carnivores**, such as *Albertosaurus*, hunted plant-eating dinosaurs, such as *Euoplocephalus* and *Styracosaurus*. These dinosaurs grazed on the area's lush plant life. Then, 65 million years ago, dinosaurs around the world suddenly died out. Scientists are not sure why this happened. Some believe a massive flood may have killed the dinosaurs. Others think that a huge **meteorite** might have hit Earth, hurling dust into the sky and blotting out the Sun. In the area around what is now Dinosaur Provincial Park, the bodies of many dinosaurs became fossils. The dinosaur fossils remained buried underground for millions of years.

■ The small, bird-like dinosaur called *Troodon* once lived in the area that is now Dinosaur Provincial Park. A model helps scientists imagine what this dinosaur may have looked like.

Site Science

After a dinosaur died, its body was covered by layers of mud and sand. Over time, these layers built up. The weight of the upper layers pressed down on the lower layers, turning the mud and sand into rock. **Minerals** from water in the ground seeped into the dinosaur's bones, teeth, claws, and horns. These parts turned to stone, creating fossils.

Dinosaur fossils stayed buried in the ground for millions of years. Over time, changes to the landscape brought the fossils in Dinosaur Provincial Park to the surface. About 20,000 years ago, glaciers flowed through the area. These massive bodies of ice scraped away the layers of rock above the fossils. As the glaciers melted, the water helped wash the rock away. Fossils that were once underground began to show through the dirt. Since then, erosion from wind and rain has helped uncover more fossils.

■ More than 300 fossilized dinosaur skeletons have been found in Dinosaur Provincial Park.

FIND MORE ONLINE

See how fossils form by clicking on "Making Fossils" at www.bbc.co.uk/sn/prehistoric_life/dinosaurs.

Becoming a World Heritage Site

Joseph Burr Tyrrell was the first person to find dinosaur bones in what is now Dinosaur Provincial Park. Tyrrell worked for the Canadian government. He surveyed the Red Deer River Valley in 1884. While there, Tyrrell was frightened by a strange skull sticking out of the hillside. It was the fossil of an *Albertosaurus*. This discovery quickly brought many people to the area. Scientists came to study the site and its fossils. Collectors searched for fossils to display in museums. To protect the site, the Alberta government made it a provincial park on June 27, 1955.

Protecting Dinosaur Provincial Park is important. The site is home to fossils made by more than 60 different types of plants and animals that lived in the area 75 million years ago. These fossils are very well preserved. This makes Dinosaur Provincial Park one of the most important dinosaur fossil beds in the world. Many rare plants and animals also live in the park today. UNESCO believes these features should be protected. They made Dinosaur Provincial Park a World Heritage Site on October 26, 1979.

■ Dinosaur fossil experts Phil Currie and his wife Eva Koppelhus have uncovered many fossils in Dinosaur Provincial Park.

Heritage Heroes

Charles M. Sternberg was born in Kansas. He was the second son of Charles H. Sternberg, a well-known fossil collector from the United States. Charles, Jr. learned how to **excavate** fossils from his father. He and his brothers, George and Levi, often worked with Charles, Sr. on important fossil-collecting projects.

In 1910, the family moved to Canada. The Canadian government hired the Sternbergs to excavate fossils in the Alberta badlands. Over the next few years, they made many important discoveries. When his father and brothers returned to the United States, Charles, Jr. stayed in Canada. He worked for the Geological Survey of Canada and the National Museum of Canada.

Charles discovered many new species of dinosaurs in the Alberta badlands. His discoveries brought a great deal of attention to the area. When he saw fossils being sold to museums and collectors outside of Canada, Charles became concerned. He believed these treasures should stay in Canada. With the help of his friend, Dr. Winfred George Anderson, Charles convinced the Alberta government to create Dinosaur Provincial Park.

Sternberg helped plan the boundaries of Dinosaur Provincial Park.

World Heritage in
CANADA

There are more than 800 UNESCO World Heritage Sites in 138 countries around the globe. Canada has 14 of these sites. Seven are natural sites, and seven are cultural sites. Each is believed to be of outstanding heritage value to all people around the world. Look at the map. Are any of these sites near your home? Have you visited any of them? Learn more about World Heritage Sites in Canada by visiting www.pc.gc.ca/progs/spm-whs/itm2-/index_e.asp.

Old Town Lunenburg (Nova Scotia)
- The best-preserved example of a planned British settlement in North America

SGang Gwaay (British Columbia)
- The site of a 2,000-year-old village that was once home to the Kunghit Haida Aboriginal People
- Contains totem poles and other key cultural objects representing the Haida way of life

Waterton Glacier International Peace Park (Alberta and Montana)
- The world's first international peace park
- Honours the peace that exists between Canada and the United States

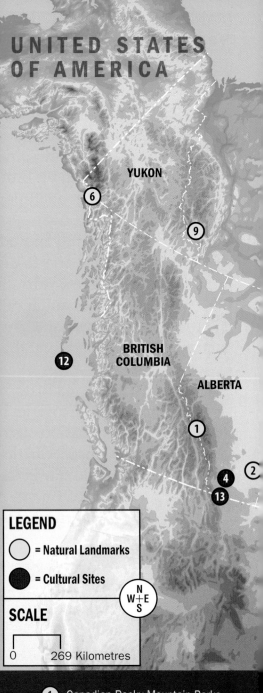

UNITED STATES OF AMERICA

YUKON

6

9

12

BRITISH COLUMBIA

ALBERTA

1

2

4

13

LEGEND
◯ = Natural Landmarks

● = Cultural Sites

N
W + E
S

SCALE

0　　　　269 Kilometres

1　Canadian Rocky Mountain Parks (Alberta and British Columbia)

2　Dinosaur Provincial Park (Alberta)

3　Gros Morne National Park (Newfoundland and Labrador)

4　Head-Smashed-In Buffalo Jump (Alberta)

CANADA

NORTHWEST
TERRITORIES

NUNAVUT

(14)

SASKATCHEWAN

NEWFOUNDLAND
AND LABRADOR

(7)

MANITOBA

(3)

PRINCE
EDWARD
ISLAND

ONTARIO

QUEBEC

(8)

NEW
BRUNSWICK

NOVA
SCOTIA

(5)

(10)

UNITED STATES
OF AMERICA

(11)

5 The Historic District of
Old-Quebec (Quebec)

6 Kluane/Wrangell-St Elias/Glacier
Bay/Tatshenshini-Alsek (British
Columbia, Yukon, and Alaska)

7 L'Anse aux Meadows National
Historic Site (Newfoundland
and Labrador)

8 Miguasha National Park (Quebec)

9 Nahanni National Park Reserve
(Northwest Territories)

10 Old Town Lunenburg (Nova Scotia)

11 Rideau Canal (Ontario)

12 SGang Gwaay (British Columbia)

13 Waterton Glacier International
Peace Park (Alberta and Montana)

14 Wood Buffalo National Park
(Alberta and Northwest Territories)

Natural Wonders

Dinosaur Provincial Park is home to the largest area of badlands in Canada. The badlands are known for their strangely shaped hoodoos. These tall pillars of rock have been worn down by wind and rain. On top of each hoodoo sits a caprock. This is a circular cap that juts out above the pillar. The caprock is made from a harder type of rock than the pillar, and it does not erode as quickly. Over time, the pillar wears down so much that the caprock falls off.

Plants, such as prickly pear cactus, sand grass, and sneezeweed, are found in the park's badlands. Rattlesnakes, scorpions, and black-widow spiders also make their homes there. More plants and animals live near the Red Deer River. The area is well known for its giant plains cottonwood trees. These trees provide an important **habitat** for many animals. About 160 types of birds, from golden eagles to house wrens, live in the park year round or part time. Visitors may also spot deer, cottontail rabbits, and pronghorn antelope. Great horned owls, bats, and coyotes come out at night.

Prairie rattlesnakes are common in Dinosaur Provincial Park.

FIND MORE ONLINE

Learn more about prairie rattlesnakes at www.canadian geograhica.ca/cgkids/animal/2005_08.asp.

Creature Feature

Albertosaurus lived in what is now Alberta 75 million years ago. It walked on two legs, like its fierce relative, *Tyrannosaurus rex*. *Albertosaurus* had a large head and short arms. Full grown, the dinosaur was about 9 metres long and 3.5 metres tall at the hip. It weighed 2,500 kilograms.

Albertosaurus was the first fossil to be found in what is now Dinosaur Provincial Park. It was also the first carnivorous dinosaur found in North America. Scientists believe that *Albertosaurus* ate mostly plant-eating dinosaurs. When no live food could be found, *Albertosaurus* fed on animals that were already dead. The dinosaur had powerful jaws that it used to snatch its prey. With its many sharp teeth, *Albertosaurus* could tear off large chunks of flesh and swallow them whole. Groups of *Albertosaurus* fossils have been found together near Dinosaur Provincial Park. For this reason, scientists believe *Albertosaurus* lived and hunted in packs.

■ *Albertosaurus* was officially named in 1905, the same year Alberta became a province.

Cultural Treasures

For thousands of years, the land near what is now Dinosaur Provincial Park has been home to the Blackfoot people. The Blackfoot are a **First Nations** group that once followed a way of life centred on hunting bison. Today, the Blackfoot are made up of three different **clans**. They are the Siksika (Blackfoot), the Kainai (also called the Blood), and the Piikani (Peigan). Many Blackfoot continue to live on **reserve lands** near Dinosaur Provincial Park, such as the Siksika reserve near Gleichen, Alberta.

Before settlers came to Alberta, the Blackfoot were great hunters and fierce warriors. They drove other First Nations groups from the land. They were also natural explorers. The Blackfoot knew of the dinosaur bones in what is now Dinosaur Provincial Park. They believed these bones were the remains of bison ancestors. The Blackfoot honoured these remains, offering them gifts and asking them for help during hunts.

■ **The Blackfoot first obtained horses around 1730. Horses made travelling and hunting easier. The Blackfoot soon became well known for their skill on horseback.**

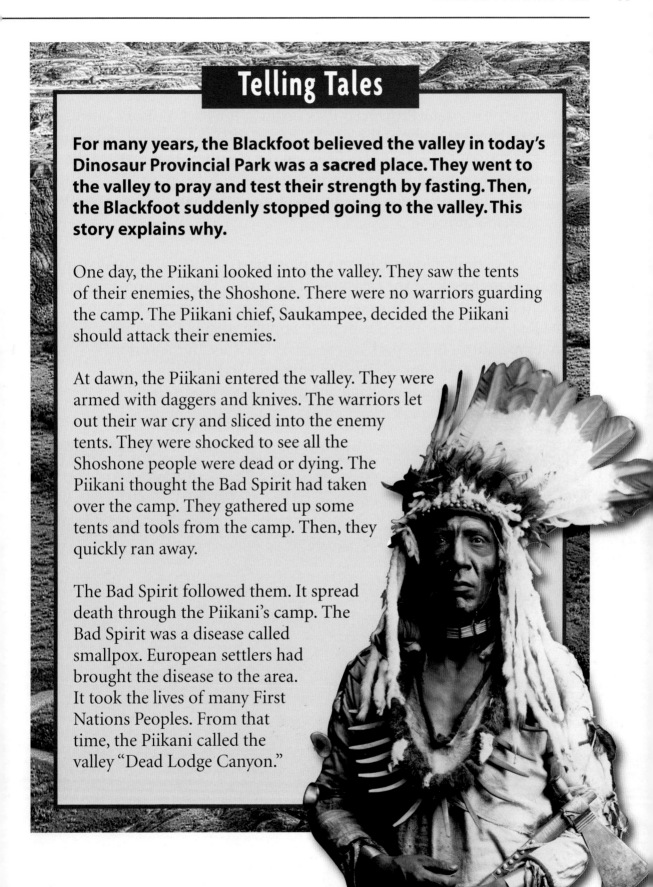

Telling Tales

For many years, the Blackfoot believed the valley in today's Dinosaur Provincial Park was a sacred place. They went to the valley to pray and test their strength by fasting. Then, the Blackfoot suddenly stopped going to the valley. This story explains why.

One day, the Piikani looked into the valley. They saw the tents of their enemies, the Shoshone. There were no warriors guarding the camp. The Piikani chief, Saukampee, decided the Piikani should attack their enemies.

At dawn, the Piikani entered the valley. They were armed with daggers and knives. The warriors let out their war cry and sliced into the enemy tents. They were shocked to see all the Shoshone people were dead or dying. The Piikani thought the Bad Spirit had taken over the camp. They gathered up some tents and tools from the camp. Then, they quickly ran away.

The Bad Spirit followed them. It spread death through the Piikani's camp. The Bad Spirit was a disease called smallpox. European settlers had brought the disease to the area. It took the lives of many First Nations Peoples. From that time, the Piikani called the valley "Dead Lodge Canyon."

Amazing Attractions

Most visits to Dinosaur Provincial Park begin at the Park Visitor Centre. Displays teach visitors about the site. Some describe the animals and plants that live in the park today. Others focus on the creatures that roamed the land million of years ago. Fossils are part of many of these displays. Through a window, visitors can watch as scientists clean and repair dinosaur fossils in the on-site laboratory.

Outdoors, five trails allow visitors to explore parts of the park. Fossil displays along the trails highlight the treasures of each area. Many visitors take guided hikes and bus tours to see the park's protected areas. Others take canoe rides on the Red Deer River. This is especially popular during the summer months, when temperatures in the park can reach 35° Celsius. In the summer, outdoor theatre programs are used to entertain and educate visitors. A 126-site campground is available for those who want to spend a few days exploring the park.

▬ **Visitors can hike for hours exploring the park's natural scenery.**

Featured Attraction

John Ware was an African-American rancher. He came to Alberta from the United States in 1882, after being freed from **slavery**. Around 1902, John moved to a ranch on the Red Deer River, near today's Dinosaur Provincial Park. He built a cabin. After John's death in 1905, the cabin was abandoned. It survived for many years, until it was moved into Dinosaur Provincial Park in the late 1950s. During the 1990s, the cabin was completely **restored**. Today, displays in the cabin tell about John's experiences as a slave, and his life after coming to southern Alberta. They present stories of John's skill with horses and his remarkable physical strength, for which he was well known.

Issues in Heritage

Dinosaur Provincial Park is well protected, but it faces some challenges. In 1990, about 40,000 people visited the park. Now, the park hosts about 90,000 visitors each year. This has caused some problems. Off-trail hiking has cut deep paths into the badlands landscape. Vehicles travelling through the park have killed many rattlesnakes. Park staff are using education, site repair, and wildlife research to help stop these problems.

The biggest concern at Dinosaur Provincial Park is fossil theft. In Alberta, it is illegal to take fossils without permission. This is true both inside and outside of provincial and national parks. Only scientists can receive special permission to take fossils for study. Visitors to Dinosaur Provincial Park are warned not to steal fossils, but many do not listen. They scoop up fossils when guides are not nearby, or enter restricted areas of the park to steal fossils. To stop people from stealing fossils, **conservation officers** patrol the park.

It is a crime to cut, damage, or remove any plant, rock, or fossil from Dinosaur Provincial Park.

FIND MORE ONLINE

Help protect World Heritage Sites at **http://whc.unesco. org/education**.

Should visitors be allowed to explore Dinosaur Provincial Park without a guide?

YES	NO
Dinosaur Provincial Park is made up of public land that everyone should be allowed to share.	Without a guide, visitors may easily become lost in the badlands. For those not familiar with the area, steep slopes, dangerous cliffs, sharp rocks, and extreme heat can be safety hazards. 
 With more people searching the ground, more fossils may be found. This could lead to exciting discoveries.	Visitors may accidentally or purposely harm fossil sites. Important clues to the past might be lost forever.
The more people can explore the park, the more interest they will have in protecting the area for the future.	 Visitors already have free access to large areas of the park, with interesting things to see and learn.

Think about this issue. Are there any possible solutions that would satisfy both sides of the debate?

Make Your Own Fossils

There are many types of fossils. Two of the most common are imprint and cast fossils. Imprint fossils are made when a dinosaur's remains decay, leaving only the shape of the dinosaur in the surrounding rock. Cast fossils are created when dinosaur remains are replaced by minerals that fill in the space left by the decayed dinosaur. Follow the steps below to create your own imprint and cast fossils.

Materials Needed
Air-dry or oven-bake clay, a small object (such as a pinecone or a plastic toy), petroleum jelly

1 To make an imprint fossil, coat the object in petroleum jelly. This will keep it from sticking to the clay when you make the imprint.

2 Roll two pieces of clay into thick, flat circles. Press the object into one of the clay circles. Lay the other clay circle on top. Press it down so the object is completely surrounded by clay.

3 Carefully remove the clay. Let it dry. The shape you see in the clay is the imprint fossil.

4 Once the imprint has completely dried, you can make a cast fossil. Take the two halves of your imprint fossil and coat them with petroleum jelly.

5 Gently press a ball of soft clay about the size of the original object into one half of the imprint. Press the other half down on top.

6 Carefully remove the clay from the imprint. It should look like the object you used to create the imprint fossils. Let the clay dry. You have made a cast fossil.

Quiz

1. True or false? Dinosaur Provincial Park is known for its pine trees.
2. When did dinosaurs live in Dinosaur Provincial Park?
3. True or false? Visitors to the park can tour the home of Charles M. Sternberg?
4. When did Dinosaur Provincial Park become a World Heritage Site?
   a. 1955   b. 1958
   c. 1962   d. 1979
5. Who discovered the first fossil in what is now Dinosaur Provincial Park?

ANSWERS: 1. False. The park is known for its giant plains cottonwood trees. 2. Seventy-five million years ago   3. False. The home of John Ware is found in the park.   4. d. 1979   5. Joseph Burr Tyrrell

Further Research

You can find more information about Dinosaur Provincial Park at your local library or on the Internet.

Libraries

Most libraries have computers that connect to a database for researching information. If you input a key word, you will be provided with a list of books in the library that contain information on that topic. Non-fiction books are arranged numerically, using their call number. Fiction books are organized alphabetically by the author's last name.

Websites

Plan a trip to Dinosaur Provincial Park at
http://tprc.alberta.ca/parks/dinosaur.

Discover Blackfoot culture at
www.glenbow.org/blackfoot.

Glossary

badlands: dry regions where wind and rain have worn rocks into strange shapes and where few plants live

carnivores: animals that eat meat

clans: groups of people that share common ancestors

conservation officers: people who enforce laws that protect land, wildlife, and other things found in nature

culture: the characteristics, beliefs, and practices of a racial, religious, or social group

excavate: to remove or uncover something by digging

First Nations: members of Canada's Aboriginal community who are not Inuit or Métis

fossil: the remains of a plant or animal from the past that has been preserved in earth or rock

habitat: the place where an animal or plant naturally lives or grows

hoodoos: strangely-shaped pillars of soft rock topped by slabs of harder rock

meteorite: a piece of matter that travels through space and reaches Earth's surface

minerals: substances found in nature that are not animals or plants

preserved: protected from injury, loss, or ruin

reserve lands: lands set aside by the Canadian government for First Nations Peoples to live on

restored: returned to its original state

sacred: connected to God or a god

slavery: a system under which people are deprived of their freedom and forced to work for others

species: groups of plants or animals that share the same characteristics

urbanization: the movement of people out of the countryside and into cities

Index